MONEY.
MONEY.
MONEY.

ACTIONS FOR
EFFECTIVE FUNDRAISING

JULES GLANZER

Cover Design: Chrissy Glanzer
Interior Design: Chrissy Glanzer
Interior Edits: Brent M. Nudo

ISBN: 0-9788585-6-8

Printed in the United States of America

ABOUT THE AUTHOR

Jules Glanzer is called many things. For almost 14 years many called him Mr. President while he served his alma mater, Tabor College, in that role. To some, he was Dr. Glanzer both as college president and seminary dean at George Fox University prior to serving at Tabor College. Others call him Dr. J, but not because of his basketball skills. Religious types are known to call him Rev. Glanzer. And some still call him Pastor Jules from 25 years of pastoring and church planting. But to most he is just Jules, a ragamuffin leader with a visionary and creative action oriented style, who is dedicated to serving and influencing people helping them grow and become all that God intended them to be. He is committed to living a God-arranged life by *honoring and trusting God with his life by being a person of influence, inspiring and impacting with relevance and integrity the lives of those who will influence others... one person at a time.* He loves his family (wife Peg, and three grown children, all of them are married, and nine grandchildren), sports (especially college sports), and baseball (an avid Astros fan). If you want to push his button and end up talking hours with him, just mention the word leadership or stewardship. He believes that everything hinges on leadership and that all of life is a stewardship entrusted to us. While serving as president of Tabor College, the constituents contributed over $53 million with no gift over $2 million. The result of this broad generosity was major capital expansion and increased curbside appeal of the campus. Jules has retired from the presidency and continues to fulfill his mission as an adjunct professor, author, mentor, and senior consultant with The Timothy Group.

ACKNOWLEDGEMENT

When I assumed the presidency, I was like a minor league Single A baseball pitcher suddenly asked to be the starting pitcher in the major leagues. I had studied leadership, but knew absolutely nothing about fundraising. To the rescue came Pat McLaughlin, founder and principal of The Timothy Group. He became our advancement consultant and my personal mentor. His ideas and what he taught me about raising money are like footprints throughout the pages of this book. I am forever grateful to God for Pat and his friendship and mentorship.

DEDICATION

Peg – my wife who heard umpteen presentations and often was there engaging the spouse.

People of Tabor College – the advancement staff, administration, faculty, coaches, and staff who helped raise $53 million reshaping the campus and college.

Tabor College constituents – who generously gave of their hard earned dollars.

TABLE OF CONTENTS

INTRODUCTION

No mother holding her newborn child prays they will grow up to be a fundraiser. Most people are filled with fear of the thought that they would be required to ask for money. Fundraising is outside the comfort zone of most people. Yet, every leader knows that money increases your impact and money is required for all projects to be successful. And in the non-profit world, and in Christian ministry, without money, the vision does not become a reality and the mission is never accomplished. As someone has said, "The only thing that counts is the mission and the money to pay for it." No margin. No mission.

Leaders in kingdom-seeking God-honoring organizations believe that their mission comes from God and that He is the one who moves the hearts of people to give, providing the margin needed to accomplish the mission. They see their role as a partnership with the Lord Jesus Christ himself in fulfilling the calling placed on their lives and the organizations they lead.

For 13½ years I had the joy of serving as the president of my alma mater, Tabor College. I learned quickly that all college presidents are bi-vocational fundraisers. The role requires that one leads the college and its many stakeholder groups while at the same time raises the needed funds for the success of the college. And to my surprise I discovered that fundraising can be a very enjoyable and rewarding experience. All non-profit CEOs, like college presidents, are bi-vocational fundraisers.

The purpose of this book is to provide simple actions and biblical stewardship insights that will help the reader in doing their part in the holy partnership they are engaged in with the Lord himself. Creating an environment, setting the stage, providing the reason, are our responsibility in the holy partnership of raising funds for the ministries we are leading. We are responsible to make wise choices, good decisions, helpful actions, and clear communication in presenting the vision and need. But we depend on the Lord to move the hearts of people to give. There are disciplines that need to be followed, questions that are helpful, and methods that produce results. But in the end, for kingdom-seeking God-honoring organizations, the results come from the Lord.

A HOLY PARTNERSHIP

For we are co-workers in God's service; you are God's field, God's building.

I Corinthians 3:9

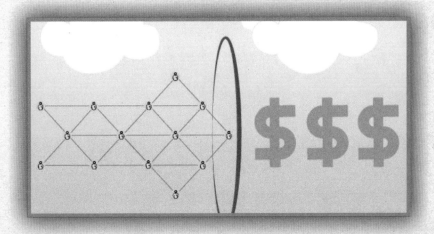

Our actions partnered with the Spirit of the Lord result in gifts furthering the mission of God in the world.

Angel, must I give again, I ask in dismay.

And must I keep giving and giving and giving it away?

Oh no, said the angel, his glance pierced me through.

Just keep giving 'til the Lord stops giving to you.

- Jerald Panas

Let your conversation be always full of grace,

seasoned with salt,

so that you may know how to answer everyone.

Colossians 4:6

ANSWER WHAT THE DONOR IS ASKING

Why me? Why us? Why this? Why now?

People of wealth want to know *Why*. Why should they give their money to you at this time for this project? When raising money for your cause, understand that the donor is asking four *Why* questions. Why me? Why us? Why this? Why now? As a fundraiser, your responsibility is to graciously present your cause in an attractive way, that answers these questions helping the donor understand your ministry's role in the mission of God in the world.

Why me?
Of the 7.9 billion people in the world, or the 331 million in the United States, why are you asking this person to make a gift to your cause? The answer to the question varies from donor to donor. Usually the answer lies in an affinity with the mission and vision of your ministry. Other times there is a historical reason. Sometimes it is a practical reason. And often it is simply the relationship that you have cultivated well over time. Whatever the reason, answering this question for the potential donor is paramount to receiving the gift.

Why us?

The impact of your mission in God's world is important. What is the eternal impact of your mission, vision, and strategic direction? How is the face of heaven changing because of your work and service? Why should the donor choose to support your ministry? What is unique about your ministry and how are you making a difference in this world and the next? Both the temporal and eternal dimensions of your ministry are important in answering this why.

Why this?

Answering how the project you are presenting is a part of what God is doing in the world is crucial to the donor deciding if they will become involved. Does your vision, mission, values, and strategic direction further the work of His kingdom? When the project becomes a reality, would the vision and values of the eternal be infused in society? If this project would not happen, what would be missing in the world? The anticipated outcomes of your project, both temporal and eternal, are central to the donor making a decision to make a gift.

Why now?

Urgency communicates importance. Timing is often one of the most significant factors in a successful project. When a donor hears an urgency, they are motivated to make a gift.

"Successful fundraising is the right person asking
the right prospect for the right amount for the
right project at the right time in the right way."
Stanley Weinstein

I planted the seed, Apollos watered it, but God
has been making it grow. So neither the one who
plants nor the one who waters is anything, but
only God, who makes things grow.
1 Corinthians 3:6-7

CREATE INPUT GOALS

*See the people. See the people. See the people.
See what God will do.*

In real estate, there are three factors in a successful project or purchase... Location. Location. Location. The same is true in fundraising. There are three factors in a successful campaign. See the people. See the people. See the people. And may I add a fourth... See what God will do.

For over 60 years, the institution I served as president had longed for an auditorium. Land on campus was designated for it. The board had already named it. It was part of the fundraising effort for two capital campaigns. But each time they fell short of raising the needed funds to build it.

A pre-campaign study determined there was significant pent up desire to build an auditorium, so we launched a campaign. Many voices kept telling us we would fail. Our vision was too big. The cost was too high. The facility was too extravagant. Even the board had a "go ahead and try" attitude. Throughout the campaign right up to the last $1 million

See the People
See the People
See the People
See the People
See what God will do
See the People
See the People
See the People
See what God will do
See the People
See the People

See the People
See what God will do
See the People
See the People
See what God will do
See the People
See what God will do
See what God will do
See the People
See the People
See what God will do
See the People
See the People
See the People
See the People
See the People
See the People
See the People

See the People
See what God will do

See what God will do
The Four Sees
See what God will do

See the People

See the People   See what God will do

See the People
See what God will do
See the People
See the People
See what God will do   See the People

push to pay for the entire 52,000 square foot facility debt free, we were told it could not be done. The Dedication Weekend was a huge celebration like nothing the college had ever experienced in its history. The Shari Flaming Center for the Arts was dedicated debt free. There were many factors in the success of the campaign, but the one principle we practiced diligently and religiously was what we affectionately called *"The 4 Sees." See the People. See the People. See the People. See what God will Do.*

There is no substitute for sitting down face to face with a potential donor and presenting your case asking them for a gift. Fly-ins, banquets, events, mass mailings, slick brochures, you name the means and method, nothing is as successful as sitting down, looking the donor in the eye, and communicating the purpose, the vision, the need, and making an ask.

In fundraising, measure your input goals, which you can control. The results of your goals come from the Lord moving the hearts of the people we see. We do not control their hearts and motives. At best we only influence them. The most important input goal is how many people are you seeing. That is how the holy partnership works. We make the call. God moves the hearts to give.

"*If you aim at nothing,*
you will hit it every time."
- Zig Ziglar

In their hearts humans plan their course,
but the LORD establishes their steps.
Proverbs 16:9

KNOW THE FOCUS OF THE CALL

Research. Relationship. Request.
Recognition. Recruit. Report.

We all have the same amount of time in a day. How we use it often determines how successful we are. When calling on potential donors, both your time and the time of the donor needs to be taken into consideration. Early in my fundraising activity, I would set an appointment, go spend time with the potential donor, and see where the conversation would go hoping for a good outcome. I often felt like I was not maximizing my time and possibly wasting the time of the potential donor.

My mentor, Pat McLaughlin, shed some significant light when he introduced me to the six R's of fundraising. It revolutionized my calling.

Research. The more you know about the donor, the more likely you will receive a gift. The first million dollar ask I made was for a football stadium. I made the ask and the donor said, "No." A couple of months later I was with the same donor on campus giving him a tour of the construction site hoping to at least receive a smaller gift. As we talked, he told me his wife had only seen one half of a football game and she hated football. If I had known this prior to my million dollar ask, I would have never asked for that amount. Whenever you are with a donor, listen, observe, and learn about them. Know your donors.

Relationship. Cultivating a relationship takes time. Demonstrating love to the potential donor is an important ingredient. Spending time with them, attending events together, engaging in the things that interest the donor, and simply relating to each other on a personal level is an important aspect of fundraising. Showing appreciation and genuinely caring for them and their families is essential in building a relationship. When the pandemic swept across the nation, our team spent two weeks making more than 600 calls to donors simply asking them how they were doing. Birthdays, anniversaries, holidays all are opportunities to make a connection. On Thanksgiving Day, I usually spend the first half of the day calling, texting, and emailing many of our donors thanking them for their involvement with the college. You know the relationship has reached a level of maturity when the donor contacts you. When I was in the hospital due to COVID-19, most of our major donors repeatedly called or texted me to see how I was doing. Simply put, love your donors. Wait for them to love you back.

Request. There comes a time in the relationship to make an ask. It is important to let the person know in advance you are planning to make a presentation and ask for a gift. Many people are fearful of making an ask. Some even refuse to ask. Just know if you do not make a request, you probably will not receive a gift.

Recognize. Showing recognition is tricky. Some donors seek it and thrive on it. Others want to be anonymous. Whichever the case, showing appropriate recognition to the donor for their gift is an important part of building trust. Most people think it is about being praised for the gift. I have always understood recognition as a way to build a legacy. The recognition allows future generations to see what was important to the donor. Recognition serves as a value statement for the donor. However, all donors love appreciation. Saying thank you within 48 hours of receiving a gift is a good goal. Larger gifts should receive a hand written note from the president or CEO. Staff should send thank you notes to their respective portfolios. Showing gratitude for a gift is the simplest way to recognize a donor.

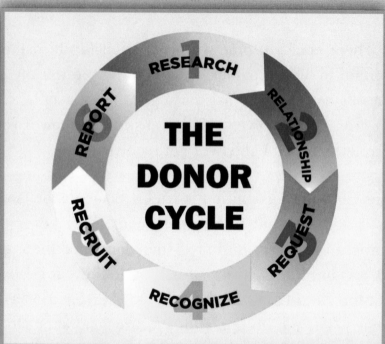

THE DONOR CYCLE

1 RESEARCH
2 RELATIONSHIP
3 REQUEST
4 RECOGNIZE
5 RECRUIT
6 REPORT

"Let's not forget the point of all this. Before each call, know which R will be the focus of your visit."

Recruit. When making a call, it is always appropriate to ask if they have any friends you could call on to make a presentation. Major donors hang out with other major donors. Asking about their friends is a great way to expand your donor base. It also is the least expensive way to engage in donor acquisition.

Report. Once your donor gives, report back to them how their gift was used and how important it was to your ministry. When our auditorium was built and we began to use it, I would often take pictures of what was happening and text them to our major donors. Reporting back to the donor demonstrates integrity and accountability to them. It increases the likelihood they will give another gift.

Following the 6 R's is a simple and effective way to plan your course of action with your donors. However, in the holy partnership, it is good to remember that the Lord is leading the way. As Stephan Joubert tweeted, "When I walk with God, He does the talking. He also determines the pace of the walking… as well as the route!" In a fundraising holy partnership, the Lord is integrally engaged in your relationship with the donor. Our responsibility is to be sensitive to His nudges, practice the 6 R's, and allow Him to arrange the various aspects of the relationship including the outcome.

"The most dangerous person is the one who listens, thinks, and observes."
- Bruce Lee

Everyone should be quick to listen, slow to speak and slow to become angry.
James 1:19

LISTEN TO YOUR DONORS

They will tell you what, when,
and how much to ask for.

When relationship is the foundation of your fundraising, it is important you listen carefully to the potential donor. In the course of time, they will tell you what they like to give to, when they could most likely make the gift, and how much they are considering. Finding out this information all comes not from asking direct questions, but simply listening to them talk.

In one instance, I called on a donor to make a request for the auditorium. After hearing my presentation, he said, "That is really not my interest. But I am interested in giving you a gift for a residence hall." Twelve months later, in the midst of a campaign for an auditorium, we dedicated a new residence hall.

In another instance, while still in the relationship phase, a donor told me about a major gift he wanted to give to another organization that refused to commit to using it in the way he intended. So he did not make the gift to them.

WHEN THEY ARE READY TO GIVE.
LISTEN: THEY WILL TELL YOU...
WHAT THEY ARE INTERESTED IN.
HOW MUCH TO ASK FOR.

When he told me the amount, I knew immediately how much to ask for when the time came for an ask.

Time is also significant. Donors often have to rearrange assets and consider tax liabilities in order to make a major gift. Appreciated assets often are the source of a major gift.

If you listen to them, they will tell you how much to ask for, when they are ready to make a gift, and what they want their hard earned dollars to impact.

"You should never be too busy to listen because it's the ultimate form of respect anyone can give a person. And donors deserve our respect."

"Be more concerned with your character than your reputation. Because your character is what you really are, while your reputation is merely what others think about you."
- John Wooden

"Whoever would love life and see good days must keep their tongue from evil and their lips from deceitful speech."
I Peter 3:10

AVOID SURPRISES

Scheduling the ask.

I was looking for a part-time job to supplement my church planter income. Back then, the "want ad" section of the newspaper was where one could find employment. I saw an ad which read, "Work as much or as little as you want. Set your own hours. Represent major brand companies like Litton, Proctor & Gamble, Sears..." and the list went on with well known companies. Call 123-456-7890. I made the call and the person insisted that he come and talk with me face to face about the employment opportunity. We set an evening when he would come by the house and explain what the job entailed.

When I went to the door, a well dressed man was standing with a tripod, 3x4 foot whiteboard, and a large briefcase. I immediately knew what he was selling... Amway. When I asked about how representing the brand names was part of the multi-level marketing plan to sell soap and cleaning supplies, he said that I had access to purchase these products at a discount for myself when I signed up. I felt deceived. I was expecting to learn about being a manufacturing representative and instead I was presented with a multi-level marketing opportunity.

Relationships are built on trust. When the foundation of fundraising is relational, the last thing you want to do is deceive the potential donor. If your friendship is genuine with the donor, you do not want to use the friendship to get a gift or employ a bait-and-switch method when you are with the donor. The way to avoid this is being clear when scheduling the meeting. Communicate to the donor, with their permission, you want to present to them a project for their consideration. Let the donor know you are seeking their involvement. Even if there is not an existing relationship, it is still advisable when calling to schedule the visit, to let the potential donor know you want to talk with them about a charitable gift opportunity. If they say no, you have saved your time and theirs. If they say yes, everyone knows this time you are going to make an ask. The donor can be mentally prepared for your conversation and have thought about how and if they want to be involved.

I have always thought that pride, greed, and deceit are the root of all other sins. When these enter a donor relationship, the relationship is doomed. Nothing will turn off a donor more than a fundraiser who thinks highly of themselves, projects an attitude of wanting more,

and comes across as untrustworthy. Humility, generosity, and integrity always gain respect and increase the potential of a gift. One might say these three positive characteristics make fundraising a God-honoring and noble profession.

Your character begins to show when scheduling the visit. I found that it is the most difficult part of the fundraising process. Jerold Panas says, "Eight-five percent of getting the gift is setting up the visit." Being honest and transparent is crucial in setting up the call. Integrity is the glue of a genuine positive relationship and an important character quality in fundraising. Trust and respect are essential in receiving a gift. When integrity, trust, and respect are broken, charitable gifts will cease. And it all begins with scheduling the call with integrity and transparency.

"Be genuinely interested in everyone you meet and everyone you meet will be genuinely interested in you."
- Rasheed Ogunlaru

The LORD would speak to Moses face to face, as one speaks to a friend.
Exodus 33:11

HAVE A PERSONAL TOUCH

Face to face is always the best.

Early in my tenure as a college president, at a dinner hosted by the Council of Christian Colleges and Universities, I happened to sit beside a seasoned president who was known for his excellent leadership and fundraising abilities. For 90 minutes, I asked questions, probed his thinking, and learned about fundraising from a college president. My major take-a-way from the conversation was that becoming a genuine friend with the donor and building the relationship with them was most important. I remember thinking, "This is not that difficult. I know how to become friends with people." From that moment on I became committed to relational fundraising rather than transactional fundraising. I saw fundraising as friend-raising.

"People give to people" is considered to be the number one rule of fundraising. When a strong, positive, and trusting relationship has been forged, donors will respond with a transformational gift. A donor trusts the ministry to the degree that they trust the messenger representing the ministry. And who the messenger is becomes critical in the response of the donor.

People are hungry for friendships. Genuine friendships where friends spent time together telling stories and loving each other is an enjoyable experience. You can gauge the depth of the friendship when the donor calls you rather than you calling them.

I have found people do not want to be treated as objects or loved because of their wealth. They desire connection. They deeply appreciate that personal touch where people are genuinely interested in what is happening in their lives.

The habit of our advancement team at the college was when an area of the country was hit by a storm or newsworthy event, we would get on the phone and call just to see how they were doing. When COVID hit, in a two week time, the team of 4 people made more than 600 calls just to see how people were doing in the pandemic. Many of these calls ended up being quite lengthy. Our team had a wonderful time and our donors deeply appreciated our love and care.

I cannot emphasize enough the importance of sitting with a potential donor face to face and talking about your ministry and their potential involvement. In this era of video conferencing, Zoom, FaceTime, and texting, there is nothing that can top sitting with a donor, in person, and discussing your project. Like God and Moses, speaking "face to face as one speaks to a friend" is the crème de la crème of fundraising.

Average fundraising close ratios as reported by

The Timothy Group with 1850+ clients are as follows:

Direct mail: 1-5% (depending on the need communicated and quality of mail piece)

Telephone: 30% (mostly with lapsed donors)

Group events: 50% (who invited them is important)

Personal request: 75-80%+ (key is right person making the call)

Pat McLaughlin, *Major Donor Game Plan.*

The personal touch is so important in receiving a sizable gift when the time is right.

"You won't get milk from a cow by sending a letter. You won't get milk by calling on the phone. The only way to get milk is to sit by its side and milk it."
- Si Seymour

I, Paul, am writing this with my own hand. I will pay it back—not to mention that you owe me your very self.

Philemon 1:19

WRITE A LETTER...
IF YOU MUST

Clear, short, and direct.

Much of Christian belief is captured in letters written many years ago. The older generation still enjoys receiving letters. A good fundraising letter is personal, focused, and motivational. There are times when a personal visit or phone call is not feasible. Usually this has to do with scale when you want to reach a large number of people with the same message simultaneously. When it is not possible to make a face to face visit or a phone call, a well crafted letter or email can produce significant results.

When writing a letter, "Say less and say it better." Make a clear opening statement that captures the donor's imagination. Paragraphs should be no longer than five or six lines with short sentences. Be direct, communicate urgency, and be personal. Write how you talk and not how your English teacher taught you to write. Answer the four *Whys*. Include a short story. Do not forget to make an ask. And add a P.S. stating what action you want the recipient to make.

Most Decembers, I receive a dozen or more fundraising letters from various charities seeking my gift. Many of them I do not read past the first paragraph. I glance at the postscript, look at the signature to see if it's real or a copy. If they have added a handwritten note, I will then go back and read the entire letter. If it is a cause that I already support, I will make a small gift, not a significant one. I assure you, if they would call on me in person, I would give a larger gift.

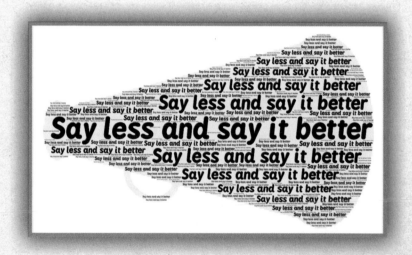

P.S. If it has to be a letter, make it clear, short, and direct.

"In every home I've known
the living room's a tomb.
In every home I've ever known,
the dining room's the room."
- Adam Gopnick

For who is greater, the one who is at the table or
the one who serves? Is it not the one who is at the
table? But I am among you as one who serves.
Luke 22:27

SELECT A COMFORTABLE PLACE

The kitchen table.

In my desire to demonstrate my courage, I asked our advancement consultant if I could take him and his wife for dinner and talk with them about making a gift to our campaign. He looked at me and said, "Have you not learned that you do not make presentations and requests in a restaurant? You make the request at the kitchen table." So we went out to dinner and then came back to their home where we sat around the kitchen table and I made the ask.

There is something magical about the kitchen table. It is a warm and comfortable place. There is equal spacial distance between all of the participants. Everyone is sitting in the same type of chair. There is privacy. You can lay your brochure, presentation device, and drink on the table. You can write on paper while making the presentation. The table is a barrier between you that does not make anyone feel like they are being exposed. The entire presentation has an informal, relational, conversational feel rather than a formal, transactional, power feel.

I have made requests in all kinds of places, from tractor cabs to hanging over the back of pickups in parking lots; from coffee shops to offices; and from text conversations to banquets. But by far, the most comfortable and successful place is the kitchen table.

Leonard Sweet in *From Tablet to Table* states, "The story of Christianity didn't take shape behind pulpits or on altars or in books. No, the story of Christianity takes shape around tables, as people face one another as equals, telling stories, sharing memories, enjoying food with one another." This is true with fundraising as well. Gifts are made as you sit around a table and share stories, sip on a drink, engage in meaningful conversation, and explore how the donor might become involved.

PROPOSAL
FOR
CHARITABLE
GIFT

"It is a balancing act for leaders to know when they should talk and when they should just listen."
- Roxi Hewertson

Ask and it will be given to you; seek and you will find; knock and the door will be opened to you.
Matthew 7:7

KNOW WHEN
TO BE SILENT

Ask, then be quiet.

There is an old fundraising saying that after making an ask, be quiet. The next person who talks, loses. If you talk, you lose the gift. If the donor talks, they lose their money.

The call I was making was to a good friend, a distant relative, and consistent donor. My mentor was with me for the visit. The donor was very generous while at the same time had a reputation of being very "tight" with his money. The donor had indicated to me on previous visits that he wanted to make a legacy gift to us. He had made an investment and had earmarked the appreciation of the investment for a charitable gift. Knowing his desire, I asked him for a million dollar gift. I was then silent. The silence lasted for 30 seconds. It did not feel like 30 seconds, it was 30 seconds.

**Silence is Golden.
Duct Tape is Silver.**

Silence
ISN'T EMPTY,
IT'S FULL OF
Answers.

Finally the donor responded. "Well you've got guts to ask me for a million dollars." The silence was broken as we all took a deep breath. My mentor said, "Sir, I wasn't sure if I should get a defibrillator for your heart." I added, "Well, I figured you would be honored that I would think you could make such a gift." We all laughed and continued to talk about his gift. What I did not know was that the investment had gone bad.

Fundraisers are used to talking. They tell stories, communicate the mission and vision they represent, and expound on the features of their project. They are answering the four *Why's*. They are salespeople working to influence donors to contribute to their cause or project. But once a request is made, they need to stop talking. I have often wondered how many gifts are reduced or not made because the fundraiser could not be silent after the ask and gave the donor an out in making a gift.

Some donors have not made a gift because they were never asked. Other donors have not made a gift because they were asked and the fundraiser asked and then talked first.

"The golden rule for every fundraiser is this: Place yourself in the donor's place."
- Unknown

"Do to others as you would have them do to you."
Luke 6:31

PRACTICE THE GOLDEN RULE

Fundraising is friend-making.

I carry in my pocket a $1 gold coin to remind me to continually practice the Golden Rule in all my relationships. In any and all circumstances, when having a hard conversation, making a purchase at a store, waiting in a customer service line, meeting with a close friend, or responding to a criticism, I work at treating them as I want to be treated in the same situation. The same is true in work relationships. Be it a peer, or someone who reports to you or the person you report to, treating each of these as you want to be treated leads to healthy relationships.

When engaged in fundraising, practicing the Golden Rule is the best advice that can be given. Treat the potential donors the way you would want to be treated. In each phase of the process from making the initial contact to securing the gift, and beyond, treat the donor as you would want to be treated if you were on the other side of the transaction. When researching the donor, building a relationship, making a request, recognizing their gift, recruiting additional donors,

and reporting the impact, act and speak in the way you would like a fundraiser to treat you. As someone has said, "No beauty shines brighter than that of a good heart."

When discussing the Golden Rule with Leonard Sweet, he talked about a variety of rules, some of which trump the golden rule.

"Iron rule: Do unto others before they do unto you.

Silver rule: Do unto others as they do unto you.

Golden rule: Do unto others as you would have them do unto you.

Platinum rule: Do unto others as they would have you do unto them.

Titanium rule: Do unto others as Jesus has done unto you."

It seems so simple, yet very difficult to treat people the way you want to be treated. But, when a gift is on the line, it becomes a whole lot easier.

"The first responsibility of leadership is to define reality. The last is to say Thank You. In between, a leader is a servant and a debtor."
- Max DePree

Remember this: Whoever sows sparingly will also reap sparingly, and whoever sows generously will also reap generously.
2 Corinthians 9:6

INFLUENCE A GIFT

Leadership is fundraising.

Leadership is influence. Leadership is an encounter between two or more people. A leader is a person you will follow to a place you could not or would not go by yourself. A leader equips and inspires people. They provide information and motivation. They appeal cognitively and emotively to people that were not able or were unwilling to go to the place they need to be.

Fundraising requires influence. Fundraising is an encounter between two or more people. A fundraiser is a person you will trust to the degree that you will make a gift. A fundraiser equips a donor with the needed information and inspires them to make a gift.

A good presentation begins with defining the reality of your situation. Usually this is stating the vision and/or the need the gift will help meet. I have found people are more drawn to a vision than a need. The bigger the vision, the more they are willing to contribute. And if it is a glaring need you are trying to meet, communicate and present it in the form of a vision that can inspire the potential donor.

When we were attempting to raise money to replace our 60 year old residence halls, we invited a major donor to campus to discuss the possibility of a gift. We took the donor on a tour showing him all the problems with the old halls and pointing out the importance of replacing them. His response was "It looks like you do not have a good maintenance plan to keep up the dorms." We had spent millions keeping up these facilities. Later, reflecting on the experience, I realized a better approach was to go to the new site where we intended to build the new residence halls and simply dream with him about what could be and talk about the kind of student living experience we wanted to provide for our students. Vision trumps need when seeking a gift.

Remember your asking for the gift is a way of serving the donor, bringing meaning to their money. There is always an exchange between you and the donor when they give a gift. Donors give for a variety of reasons: honor, fame, inner conviction, belonging, sense of duty, historical connection, tax benefits, and many more noble and worthy reasons. But most important to them is they will receive satisfaction and fulfillment from their gift. In serving your donors, you are providing them with something they are craving. We are most like Jesus when we are serving.

Plus, you owe the donor honesty, transparency, and integrity in how you communicate and use the gift once it is given. What your organization owes your donors is often overlooked or at minimum, thought silently. But when a donor makes a gift, you are obligated to them. Obligated to honor their intentions, communicate with them the significance of the gift, and affirm their generosity.

Finally, say thank you. Texting, phone calls, form letters all are ways to say thank you. But there is nothing better than a personal handwritten note thanking the donor for the gift. These notes are cherished and valued by all donors. It does not cost much to say thank you. But it could cost you a future gift if you do not say thanks.

Influence
LEADERSHIP IS
FUNDRAISING IS
Encounter between two or more
Follow to place you could not or would not go by self
equips
inspires

"The joy, satisfaction, and fulfillment of bringing meaning to money is greater than the praise and thankfulness of people."

- Unknown

"Who then is the faithful and wise manager, whom the master puts in charge of his servants to give them their food allowance at the proper time?"

Luke 12:42

BRING MEANING
TO MONEY

Fundraising is stewardship.

After 25 years serving in pastoral roles, 6½ years as a Seminary Dean, and 13½ years as a college president, I am convinced that all of life and leadership is stewardship. A stewardship of mission and vision, power and authority, people and culture, and time and resources. All of life, living, and leading is a stewardship entrusted to us by the creator of life.

Stewardship can be defined as, "Doing the right thing at the right time in the right way for the right reason." Fundraising can be defined in a similar way. A successful donor visit is when the right person asks the right person for the right amount for the right project in the right place at the right time. When this happens, the fundraiser gives the donor the best gift possible. They have provided what the donor has wanted all along. The donor has received the gift of meaning. You have brought meaning to their money.

Fundraising is...

RIGHT THING
Right project
Right time
Right reason
Right person
Right reason
Right reason
Right time
Right project
Right time
Right amount
Right time
RIGHT THING
Right place
Right time
Right amount
Right place
Right amount
Right project

Right time
Right person
Right place
Right time
Right time
Right person
Right person
Right way
Right way
Right place
RIGHT THING
Right way
Right way
Right reason
Right way
Right time
Right project
Right time
Right amount
Right person
Right place
Right amount
Right amount

Right reason
RIGHT THING

Stewardship is...
RIGHT THING
Right person
RIGHT THING
Right person

Dale Carnegie in *How to Win Friends and Influence People* describes it well. "Personally I am very fond of strawberries and cream, but I have found that for some strange reason, fish prefer worms. So when I went fishing, I didn't think about what I wanted. I thought about what they wanted. I didn't bait the hook with strawberries and cream. Rather, I dangled a worm or grasshopper in front of the fish and said: 'Wouldn't you like to have that?'"

Often ministries set a goal for how much they want to raise. They create brochures and write letters. The staff hits the road excited about the goal, asking donors to help them reach the goal. Maybe it is just me, but I have always reacted negatively when I, as a donor, am asked to help reach a goal. My preference is to give to a vision or mission rather than an arbitrary goal set by the advancement team. Setting goals is important, but good bait inspires donors to contribute to your vision.

When attempting to influence a potential donor to make a gift, understanding what the donor appreciates, enjoys, and their passion and interest, is practicing stewardship.

PERSONAL ACTION

We make a living by what we get. We make a life by what we give.
- Winston Churchill

The best fundraisers are those who practice philanthropy themselves. As a Christ-follower, I have come to the conviction that…

- Everything we have and are belongs to God.
- We live and give in response to God.
- We are happiest and most fulfilled when we give.

That means…

- As a child of God, everything I have belongs to Him.
- As my Heavenly Father, He is responsible to take care of His children.
- That makes me a steward of all that He has given me.

When talking with people about making a gift, I am convinced, even before a presentation is made…

- That their generous response will bring joy and happiness to their lives.
- That making a gift demonstrates their stewardship.
- That generosity, gratitude, and graciousness are the three big G's of a life well lived.

Give, and it will be given to you. A good measure, pressed down, shaken together and running over, will be poured into your lap. For with the measure you use, it will be measured to you."
Luke 6:38

CORPORATE ACTION

"Culture eats strategy for lunch."
- Peter Drucker

While president of Tabor College, we intentionally shaped a fundraising culture. Here are a dozen actions that intentionally shaped our fundraising practices.

1. We focus on face to face and voice to voice contacts.

2. We do not spend a lot of money to raise a lot of money.

3. We communicate often with each other.

4. We are relationship-driven not event-driven.

5. We present vision as a way to communicate need.

6. We are not afraid to ask.

7. We set big goals.

8. We maximize our time and effort.

9. We encourage good biblical stewardship.

10. We practice Max DePree's famous leadership statement:
    a. We define reality for our donors.
    b. We serve them.
    c. We know what we owe them.
    d. We say thank you.

11. We listen to the donors and honor their wishes.

12. We do not take no from a person who cannot give us a yes.

Good will come to those who are generous and lend freely,
who conduct their affairs with justice.
Psalms 112:5

BIBLICAL ACTION

Bring the whole tithe into the storehouse, *that there may be food in my house. "Test me in this," says the LORD Almighty, "and see if I will not throw open the floodgates of heaven and pour out so much blessing that there will not be room enough to store it." Malachi 3:10*

Do not store up for yourselves treasures on earth, *where moths and vermin destroy, and where thieves break in and steal. But* **store up for yourselves treasures in heaven**, *where moths and vermin do not destroy, and where thieves do not break in and steal. For where your treasure is, there your heart will be also. Matthew 6:19-21*

On the first day of every week, each one of you should **set aside a sum of money** *in keeping with your income, saving it up, so that when I come no collections will have to be made. 1 Corinthians 16:2*

But since you excel in everything —in faith, in speech, in knowledge, in complete earnestness and in the love we have kindled in you—see that you also **excel in this grace of giving.** *2 Corinthians 8:7*

Remember this: Whoever sows sparingly will also reap sparingly, and whoever sows generously will also reap generously. Each of you should **give what you have decided in your heart to give,** *not reluctantly or under compulsion, for God loves a cheerful giver. 2 Corinthians 9:6-7*

Command them to **do good,** *to* **be rich in good deeds,** *and to* **be generous and willing to share.** *1 Timothy 6:18*

Honor the LORD with your wealth, *with the firstfruits of all your crops; Proverbs 3:9*

Keep your lives free from the love of money *and be content with what you have, because God has said,"Never will I leave you; never will I forsake you." Hebrews 13:5*